Romans, gladiators and games

2nd Edition

THE ROMAN WORLD OF THE FIRST CHRISTIANS

BRIAN EDWARDS AND CLIVE ANDERSON

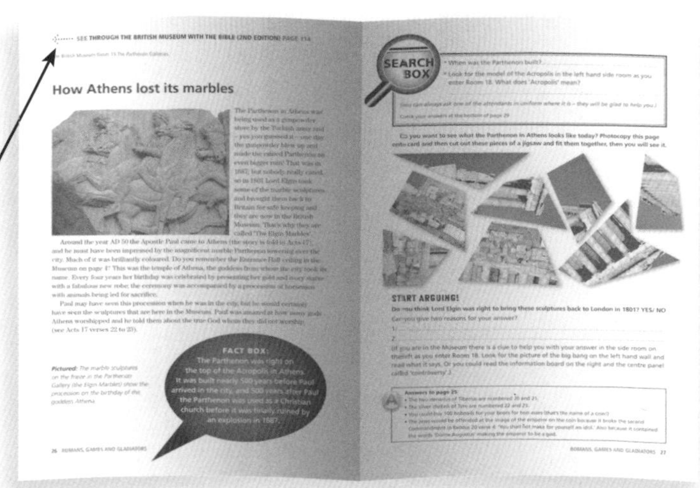

LOOK OUT FOR THIS!

Throughout the book you will see this at the top of each page: See THROUGH THE BRITISH MUSEUM WITH THE BIBLE (3RD EDITION) pages **If you have a copy of Through the British Museum with the Bible it will help you to explore Romans, gladiators and games in more detail.**

Through the British Museum with the Bible is available from Day One Publications.

DayOne

Join us in the British Museum

The British Museum is London's number one visitor attraction

- Six million people from all over the world come here every year.
- Who wants to spend their holidays in a museum?
- Seventy thousand items on display. How do you know what to look at?
- What does the British Museum have anything to do with the Bible?

Whether you live hundreds of miles away or just round the corner:

Welcome to the British Museum

Pictured: *The front of the British Museum in London with its great columns copying the architecture of ancient Greece.*

Web addresses of the British Museum for families and children are **www.britishmuseum.org/visiting/family_visits** and **www.britishmuseum.org/explore/young_explorers1**. You will find these very helpful.

Each double page has an interesting **FACT BOX** like this:

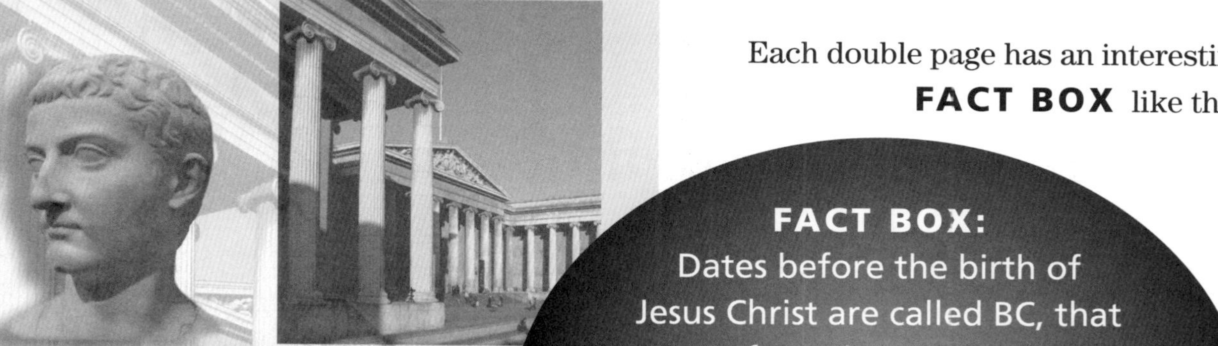

FACT BOX:
Dates before the birth of Jesus Christ are called BC, that means 'Before Christ'. Dates after his birth are called AD, and that is short for the Latin words *anno domini* which means 'in the year of our Lord'. BC is put after the date and AD is put before it, like this: 31 BC. AD 70.

If you are in the museum each double page has a **SEARCH BOX** which will get you hunting for interesting things and answering fascinating questions.

HOW TO FIND A VERSE IN THE BIBLE

When we refer to a Bible verse it will look like this: Luke 2 verse 1. To find it, look up Luke in the index at the front of your Bible, that will give you the page number where Luke starts. Then turn to chapter two and find the first verse. All the verses are numbered. We are using the New International Version *of the Bible.*

HOW TO FIND SOMETHING IN THE MUSEUM

We might say something like this: 'in Room 70 go to *case 7 no.13.'* If you see a room number over a door, that's the room you are in and not the one you are about to enter. Then look for the number on the display cases. Usually at the top left or right corner. Then, many items will have a number by them.

Not all items are in cases, but they are all very old and valuable so please **don't touch** any of them.

See **THROUGH THE BRITISH MUSEUM WITH THE BIBLE (3RD EDITION)** pages 17 and 21-23

The British Museum: Victorian Entrance Hall, Great Court and Reading Room.

Ancient — and very modern

Some of the things in the British Museum are more than seven thousand years old, and some are very new. The Great Court is the same size as a football pitch and if you're standing in it right now, watch out because there's 80 tons of glass and steel above you — that's about the same weight as 160 African elephants!

However, you have already walked through something much older. The front of the building with its huge columns was built in 1852 — the year after the Great Exhibition. Did you look up when you first entered the building? Go and take another look — or look at the centre picture of the front cover of this book. That ceiling is in the Victorian Entrance Hall, and there are sixty-five different colours up there. Most of the ancient buildings of the Persians and Greeks, were originally brightly coloured. The Parthenon, that we will visit later in this book, was once as colourful as this ceiling.

The Reading Room at the centre of the Museum is exactly the same as it was when the Victorians walked here – apart from the computers! Many famous people have worked in this library. You can use a computer to search for items in the Museum and even order a picture of your favourite exhibit and collect it before you leave for home.

***Pictured:** The Reading Room was first opened in 1857 and many famous people have studied here.*

FACT BOX:
Five hundred years ago many of our churches and cathedrals were also brightly coloured inside, with pictures painted on the walls.

SEARCH BOX

In the Reading Room make a note of **three** of the famous people whom you have heard of that have used this library in the past. There is a list of them to your right and left just inside the entrance to the Room. What were they famous for?

Famous person	Famous for
....	....
....	....
....	....

English Heritage helped to restore the beautiful ceiling of the Victorian Entrance Hall in the year 2,000, mixing the 65 different colours. Pretend you are part of that working party and colour this picture of the ceiling. You will find a picture in the centre of the front cover of this book and you can use that as your guide.

Research

If you have access to the internet, log on to the Museum website **www.thebritishmuseum.ac.uk/childrenscompass** and see if you can find any more information that we have not mentioned about the Victorian Entrance Hall, the Great Court and the Reading Room. Write the results of your research here:

British Museum Room 70 Rome: city and empire.

Winner takes all

On one side: around 300 heavy ships; the decks lined with men ready to hurl great rocks and fire arrows into the enemy squadron before ramming their ships with the huge three ton battering rams on the bow. That was the navy of Anthony and Cleopatra. But they had a problem: before the battle started, many of their oarsmen (no engines in ships in those days) had either died or were sick with malaria (an illness spread by insects)! **On the other side:** much smaller but faster ships, and with well trained and healthy oarsmen. That was Octavian's navy.

The Battle of Actium raged all day on 2 September 31 BC and in the end Octavian destroyed the fleet of Anthony and Cleopatra who both sailed off and later committed suicide.

Octavian was now in control of the Roman empire and called himself 'Caesar Augustus'.

Have you heard that name before?

'In those days Caesar Augustus issued a decree that a census should be taken of the entire Roman world' (Luke chapter 2 verse1).

That's him. It was because of that census that Mary and Joseph returned to Bethlehem, where Jesus was born.

Trendy Livia

Augustus married Livia, whose hair style many women and girls wanted to copy. She had a little knot at the front (called a *nodus*) which was connected by a braid to a bun at the back. Writing in the New Testament, Peter and Paul were probably thinking of this when they told the Christian women to avoid *'braided hair'* (1 Peter 3 verse 3 and in 1 Timothy 2 verse 9). They meant that Christians do not have to follow the fashion.

Livia's son, **Tiberius**, became emperor in AD 14 when Jesus was still a teenager. Tiberius was an angry and cruel emperor and very jealous of his mother.

Pictured top: *This is a marble bust of Augustus in the Museum. He designed amazing buildings, established a strong army, organised a police and fire service in Rome, built good roads and encouraged reading and writing. All good stuff.*

Pictured above: *Livia and her neat hair do. It was unusual for a sculpture to be made of a wife so this shows how important Livia was. Beside her is her son Tiberius.*

FACT BOX:
'Caesar' was a family name and 'Augustus' means 'the exalted'. A 'census' meant that everyone had to have their names written in a register.

* There are marble busts of ☐ Augustus, ☐ Livia and ☐ Tiberius in *Room 70.* Tick this box each time you find one of them.
* Go to *case 7 no.13.* Here is a small terracotta (clay) lamp with a portrait on it? Whose portrait is this? ....
* Now go to *case 15.* Can you find 'The sword of Tiberius'? Write down its 'accession number' (that's the special Museum number on it. This one starts with: GR.)

  Every item in the Museum has its own special accession number. GR ....

Check your answers at the bottom of page 9.

Copy the three sculptures of Augustus, Livia and Tiberius (we have given you a start so you need to match up our start with the right head). Then write under each, their name and what their relationship was to each other.

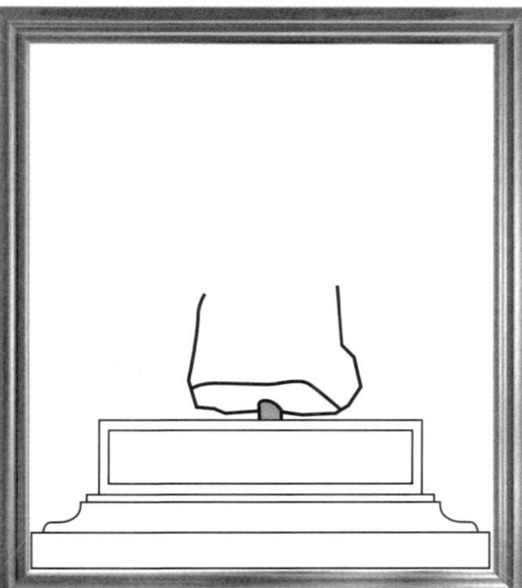

What would Tiberius think?

Why do you think Tiberius would **not** have been pleased to have his bust placed close to, and just **behind,** that of his mother?

___

___

How old was Livia when she died?

Livia married Augustus when she was 22 years old and they were married for 50 years. After Augustus died Livia lived for another 14 years. So, how old was Livia when she died?

Livia was .... when she died.

How old was Tiberius?

Tiberius was born in 42 BC. How old was he when he became emperor?
(All the information you need is on page 6)

Tiberius was .... when he became emperor.

British Museum Room 70 case 27.

Who wants to be Herod's pig?

Now where did I read this?: *'After Jesus was born in Bethlehem in Judea, during the time of King Herod, Magi from the east came to Jerusalem and asked, "Where is the one who has been born king of the Jews? We saw his star in the east and have come to worship him."'*

That's in Matthew chapter 2 verse 1.

Herod was a cruel man who murdered anyone he thought was a threat to his power — that included his wife and two of his sons. The emperor Augustus once said 'I would rather be Herod's pig than his son'!

When those wise men (Magi) told Herod that they believed the 'king of the Jews' had been born somewhere nearby, the Bible says Herod was 'disturbed, and all Jerusalem with him.' That spelt big trouble. Perhaps you know what happened next. When he learned that Bethlehem was the birth place, Herod ordered all the baby boys there to be murdered. Herod died soon after the birth of Jesus but his sons were not much better, so the Romans put their own man in charge — Pontius Pilate.

Pontius Pilate was the Governor of Judea working for the Romans, and he was the one who ordered the death of Jesus. Pilate was a bully and constantly upset the Jews; because of this he was eventually sacked.

FACT BOX:
'Herod the Great' built the city of Caesarea and some impressive public buildings, especially the magnificent temple in Jerusalem which was not finished until long after his death.

Pictured from left to right:

A bronze coin of Herod the Great. He was in charge of Judea when Jesus was born.

A bronze coin of Pilate issued at the time of the arrest and crucifixion of Jesus while Pilate controlled Palestine on behalf of the emperor Tiberius.

A coin showing Herod Agrippa and his brother at the coronation of a Roman emperor in AD 41.

In *case 27* in the centre panel you will find a coin produced by Herod the Great, one of Pilate, and another of Herod of Chalcis and his brother Herod Agrippa I. These brothers are at the coronation of a Roman emperor — what is the emperor's name?

....

It's no.4 and the writing beside it will give you the answer.

Check your answers at the bottom of page 11.

The Roman emperor once said of Herod the Great that he would rather be an animal belonging to Herod than his son. Draw a picture of the animal he had in mind.

You can read the story of Jesus on trial before Pilate in **Matthew 27 verses 11 to 26** where Pilate is called the 'governor'. He offered to release Jesus or another prisoner, and the priests and elders of Jerusalem could choose. They chose the other man.

What was his name? **B** ___ ___ ___ ___ ___ ___ ___

Answers to page 7.

- The portrait on the terracotta lamp is probably Livia.
- The accession number for The sword of Tiberius is GR 1866.8-61
- Livia was 86 years old when she died. • Tiberius was 56 years old when he became emperor.

British Museum Room 70 Rome: city and empire.

The mad butcher of Rome and other emperors

The emperor **Nero** earned the nickname: 'The mad butcher of Rome', and it's not surprising because he murdered members of his own family, including his mother, his wife — and anyone else who disagreed with him.

In AD 64 there was a devastating fire that burned out the centre of Rome. Most people believed that Nero started the fire, and to turn the blame away from himself he accused the Christians. At this time the Roman emperors began to be thought of as gods. Because Christians refused to worship the emperor, many were put to death; often by being thrown to wild animals as a sport for crowds to watch. In the New Testament Paul often found himself in prison for preaching about Jesus. He was eventually arrested for this and then sentenced to death by the emperor Nero. This was probably in the year of the fire in Rome.

When Nero died, **Vespasian** became emperor. He was a tough old soldier, and when the Jews fought against Romans he ordered his son **Titus** to destroy Jerusalem. It was a terrible siege — one of the worst in history. Thousands starved to death, and one night Titus killed 500 Jews outside the city walls to scare those still inside the city. In his teaching, Jesus warned that Jerusalem would be destroyed. (Matthew 24 verses 1 and 2). Later Titus became emperor and was known as 'Rome's golden boy' because he defeated the Jews.

Pictured: *The emperor Vespasian (right), and beside him his son Titus who as a Roman general in AD 70 destroyed Jerusalem and its temple and massacred the inhabitants.*

FACT BOX:
A 'siege' is when an army surrounds a city to force it to surrender by stopping reinforcements or food from getting in.

There is no bust of Nero in the Museum, but can you find the marble busts of Vespasian and Titus? What are their accession numbers?

Vespasian's accession number is...

Titus' accession number is...

Have you forgotten what an 'accession number' is?
Check out in the **SEARCH BOX** on page 7.

Check your answers at the bottom of page 13.

WORD SEARCH:

Can you find the names of the four emperors, and the wife of one of them, who are mentioned on pages 6 and 8?
Be warned .... three of them are spelt backwards!

A	G	N	H	B	V	C	S	O	K	M	B
M	K	L	P	L	D	E	B	Q	V	C	X
T	Y	U	N	H	I	F	C	D	X	S	A
I	O	M	N	G	T	V	C	D	Q	E	S
N	S	H	G	T	V	F	I	X	Z	A	T
P	S	U	T	S	U	G	U	A	G	T	V
T	H	N	I	B	F	V	R	C	D	I	P
Q	L	R	Y	R	H	B	G	V	C	T	D
U	K	O	M	N	E	U	H	B	T	U	H
S	D	F	G	H	J	B	B	H	T	S	R
O	R	E	N	G	V	F	I	D	J	N	H
N	F	G	B	V	C	X	L	T	G	S	Z

Now take the first letter of the three names that are spelt backwards and make the name of a tiny insect.

Which letter of the alphabet is NOT included in this word search box?

Answer to page 9.

- The emperor was Claudius. Incidentally, he was the emperor who ordered the invasion of Britain in AD 43.
- The man chosen instead of Jesus was called Barabbas.

British Museum Room 69 Greek and Roman Life. Cases 20 Gladiators and 18 Sport.

Gladiator — with a PG rating!

Every year fifty thousand gladiators, watched by more than fifty thousand spectators, would fight to the death in the Coliseum in Rome. The gladiators, who were mostly slaves, criminals or prisoners, would often draw lots to discover who they would fight in this cruel and vicious 'sport'. The winning gladiators became heroes, almost like pop idols; but the unsuccessful were usually killed. And they weren't always men, women also fought each other.

Just like a PG rating at the cinema, children could attend — provided they were accompanied by an adult!

In one of his letters to the Christians at Corinth, Paul wrote about fighting *'wild beasts in Ephesus'* (1 Corinthians 15 verse 32). This was exactly what happened to many Christians as they were thrown to the wild animals in the arena for the entertainment of the crowds just for standing up for what they believed. Eventually the shows stopped about AD 400 because so many Christians opposed them.

Boxing and wrestling

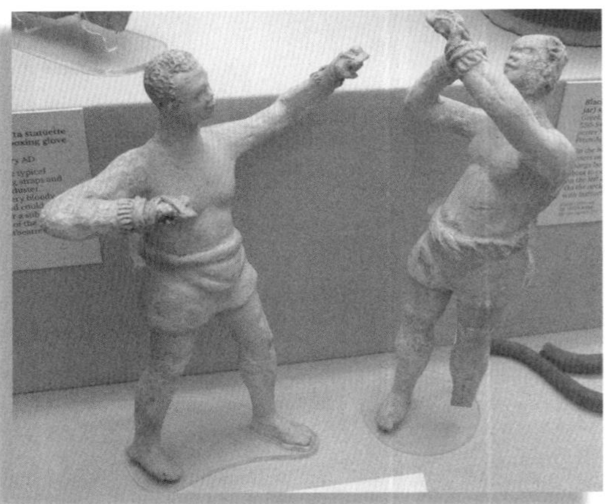

Boxing in the first century was violent. There were no rounds and no time limit. The competitors just slogged it out until one gave up or was knocked unconscious. Paul sometimes used the example of sport to describe how hard he worked for God. In 1 Corinthians 9 verse 26 he referred to boxing: *'I do not fight like a man beating the air.'* He also compared prayer to wrestling in Colossians 4 verse 11. Both boxing and wrestling were popular in the first century.

Pictured top: *A small clay relief of a gladiator fighting a lioness.*

Pictured above: *Two men boxing. Look at their hands. In the first century, boxers did not wear padded gloves; in fact, their gloves had lead balls in them to inflict very nasty wounds on the opponent.*

FACT BOX:
Our English word 'arena' comes from the Latin for 'sand'. Sand was used to cover the floor of the arena to soak up the blood.

SEARCH BOX

* Sometimes gladiators fought with animals. In *case 20* can you find part of a plaque of a contest like this?
* What is the animal leaping at the gladiator?

....

* Can you find two men boxing in *case 18*? What country did these two come from and how can you tell?

....

* Look at the pictures on the artefacts in *case 18*. What other sports can you see?

....

Check your answers at the bottom of page 15.

This is the gladiator's helmet in the museum. It would have been highly polished and a fine, colourful plume would have been at the top. Add your own plume with your favourite colours.

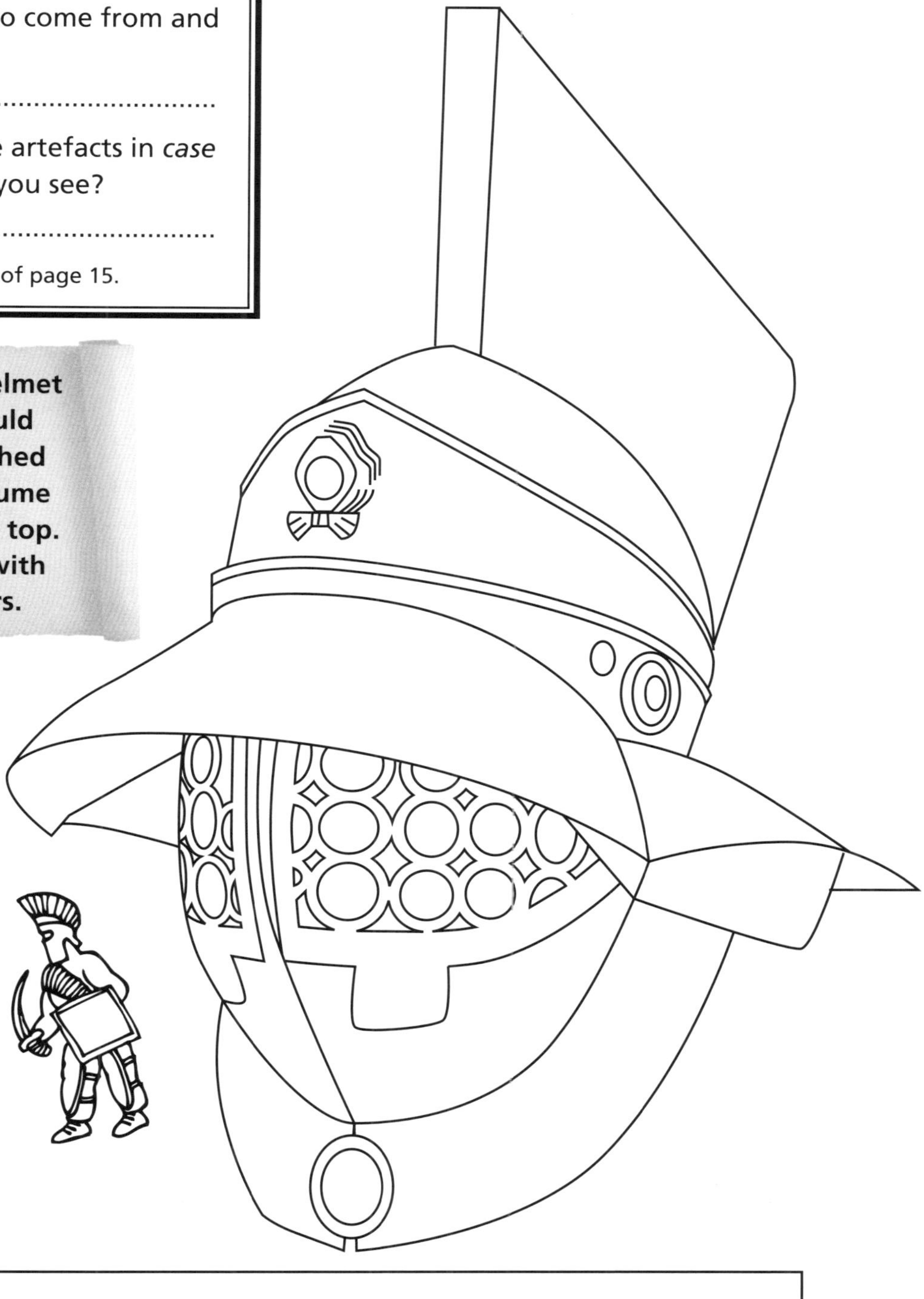

Answers to page 11

- Vespasian's accession number is GR 1850.3-4.35 • Titus' accession number is GR 1909.6-10.1
  (By the way, the first four digits tell us the year that the exhibit came into the Museum).
- Augustus, Nero, Tiberius, Titus and Livia. • The word is ANT. The missing letter is W.

British Museum Room 69 Greek and Roman Life. Case 17 The Roman Army.

Roman citizenship

Sorry girls, no lady could be a Roman Citizen!

By the time Romans invaded Britain in AD 43, Roman legions were serving from France all the way to Turkey and Egypt. They referred to Britain as 'Britannia Romana' (Roman Britain).

Although Rome could be very cruel to its enemies, there were also benefits to being under Roman rule: they kept the frontiers safe for the countries they controlled and built straight roads to make communication fast and easy. The two main languages people spoke were Latin and Greek. Above all, Roman citizenship meant you were guaranteed a fair trial in law.

Because Roman soldiers were everywhere, the New Testament often uses military language as metaphors. Here are three that we can find all in one case in Room 69:

Victory parades

In 2 Corinthians 2 verse 14 Paul claimed that those who follow Christ are in a *'triumphal procession'*. He was thinking about the Roman legions returning in triumph with their prisoners in chains. Here is a display in the Museum that illustrates this.

Swords

In Hebrews 4 verse 12 the Bible is described as a 'short two-edged sword' because it can change lives in a very powerful way! Elsewhere the Bible is called *'the sword of the Spirit'* (Ephesians 6 verse17).

Passports

Often the New Testament refers to Christians as 'citizens' of heaven: Philippians 3 verse 20 says, *'Our citizenship is in heaven.'* Although Christian slaves were not allowed to become Roman citizens they knew that they were citizens of a much better kingdom — heaven!

Pictured top: *A terracotta panel showing part of a triumphal procession with prisoners in chains.*

Pictured middle: *The ivory hilt (handle) of a short two-edged sword called a 'gladius'.*

Pictured bottom: *Part of a bronze plate awarding Roman citizenship to a soldier on his discharge from the army. This soldier had served in the cavalry in Britain.*

FACT BOX:
The short, two-edged sword called the *gladius* was used by the gladiators and the Roman legionaries. It was a deadly weapon in close combat.

In *case 17* what other forms of Roman weaponry can you find?

....

Check your answers at the bottom of page 17.

Imagine that you are a Roman soldier serving in the cavalry in *Britannia Romana;* it is December in the year AD 43 and you have just landed in Kent with the invasion force sent by the emperor Claudius. You are part of the IX Legion Hispana and your home is in Spain, though you have recently been serving in Hungary with General Plautius who is now in command of this massive invasion of Britain. The British, led by Caratacus, know the land well and are providing stiff resistance. After a battle to get across the River Medway your legion is assigned rear guard duties to watch the supply lines. Often you are sent out with a foraging party to find food locally. You have a short break to write a letter home to your mother in Spain. It's winter here, on the damp marshes of Kent.

What two things would you tell your mum that you are missing most and what two things are you most afraid of? Use the paragraph above for clues to help you.

....

....

....

....

PASSPORT TO ROME

There were three main ways you could become a Roman Citizen. To find the three words you will need to count the letters in the first paragraph on this page! Each word will be found in a complete sentence.

For example in the first sentence:
2. 13. 20. 23 = moon.

Now try it for the real answers.

In the first sentence:
52. 54. 61. 81. 82

_ _ _ _ _

In the second sentence:
7. 36. 37. 66. 85. 89. 121. 140

_ _ _ _ _ _ _ _

In the third sentence:
9. 12. 18. 49. 50. 68. 69

_ _ _ _ _ _ _

Answers to page 12
- A lioness. • They came from Africa and we know this because of their faces and short hair.
- Men wrestling are also included here.

SEE THROUGH THE BRITISH MUSEUM WITH THE BIBLE (3RD EDITION) PAGES 104-105

British Museum Room 69 Greek and Roman Life. Cases 20 Drama, and 26 Potters and carpenters.

Putting on a face

Don't be a hypocrite! That refers to a person who is pretending to be something they are not.

Jesus used the word for someone who criticises others whilst there is a lot wrong with themselves (Matthew 7 verse 5). The word 'hypocrite' meant 'a play actor' and was used of actors on the stage because they wore a mask to cover their real face and show the character they were pretending to be. They were 'two-faced'.

Light in dark places

Imagine your house on a dark night in winter with only one candle for light, and when you go out into the street there are no lights at all. That's what it was like in the time of Jesus. They didn't have candles, so people made little bowls of clay with a spout, and oil would be poured into the bowl and a wick placed in the spout — this was their lamp. In wealthy homes the bowl would have lots of 'spouts' to give more light.

The oil used in the lamps was from the seeds of the sesame plant, olive oil or even animal fat – though this was probably a bit smelly! The wick was made of flax or similar fibre or even old pieces of rag.

These are the kind of lamps that Jesus referred to in his story of the girls at the wedding *'who took their lamps and went out to meet the bridegroom'* (Matthew 25 verse1), and of the lamp *'on its stand'* giving *'light to everyone in the house'* (Matthew 5 verse 15). The lamp and its light became a symbol of joy and guidance and this is why Jesus referred to himself and his followers as *'the light of the world'* (John 8 verse 12).

Later, Christians often had their lamps stamped with the first two letters of the name 'Christ' in Greek. It looked like this and was called the 'chi-rho' symbol.

FACT BOX:
The Greek word for a mask was *hupocrites*, from which we get our word 'hypocrite'.

Pictured top: *A first century mask used in the theatre. It was made of terracotta which is baked clay. Some were even made of bronze.*

Pictured above: *A small oil lamp used in the first century.*

* In *case 26* there are lots of lamps and some of them are decorated. Can you find the mould used to make lamps with the Christian symbol on it? (The accession number is GR 1975.1–29.1).

  When was this one made? ....

* In *case 21* look for the mask that actors would use. How old is this one? ....

  What is it made of? ....

Check your answers at the bottom of page 19.

Jesus told a story about ten girls each with an oil lamp to provide light for a wedding reception. But only five were wise enough to make sure they had sufficient oil to keep their lamp bright. Can you find the five wise girls? (You can find the story in Matthew 25).

Using the grid as your guide, enlarge this picture of a very old mask that is in the British Museum so that it fits your own face.

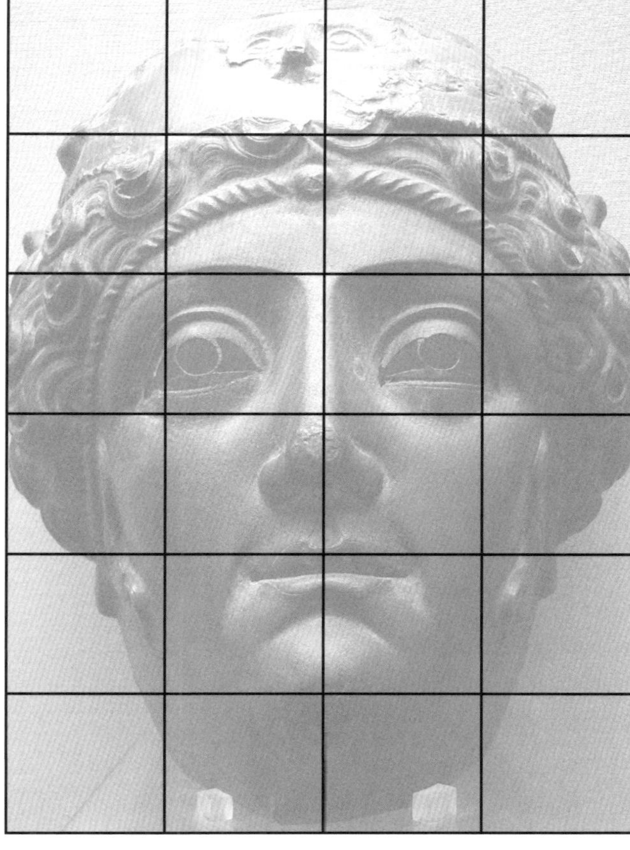

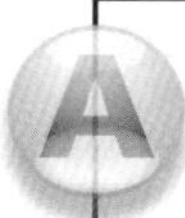

Answers to page 15

- arrow heads, iron sword and lead sling and bullet catapults.
- birth, purchase, service.

British Museum Room 69. Case 3 Medicine, case 7 Writing, and case 9 Games.

Off to the doctor

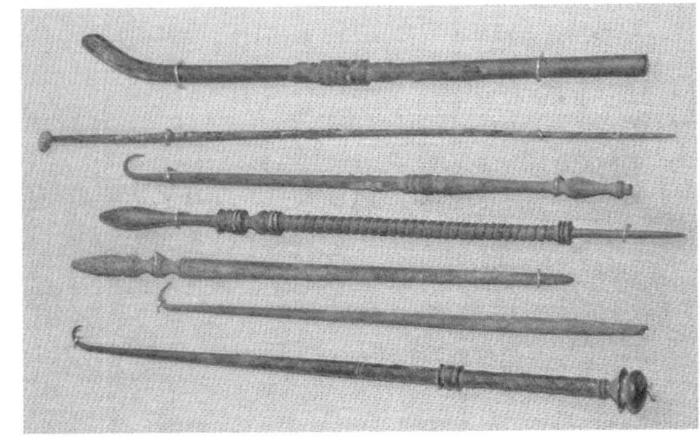

Imagine being stripped to the waist and being beaten with thirty-nine lashes of a leather whip — that happened to Paul often, just because he preached about Jesus (read 2 Corinthians 12 verse 24). Fortunately Luke, who was a doctor, went with Paul on many of his journeys. Paul also had eye problems and Luke would have some ointments for this too. In the Museum there is a display of the kind of instruments Luke would have used. There is a long surgical drill that was used to remove arrow heads. But they had very little to stop the pain and all operations were without anaesthetic!

Mirror, mirror on the wall

When you look in a mirror, you can see a very clear reflection of yourself, but in Paul's day it was not like that. Their mirrors were made from brass that was highly polished; but the reflection was not very clear. Paul once contrasted this with heaven to show that nothing here is perfect, but everything in heaven is perfect. This is how he wrote: *'Now we see but a poor reflection as in a mirror; then we shall see face to face'* (1 Corinthians 13 verse 12).

Back to school!

Even in the first century boys had to learn to read and write! They did have pens, but they didn't have paper. The pen was made of sharpened wood, the ink was probably soot mixed with gum, and the 'paper' was often a piece of broken pottery (which is called *ostracon*). The Museum has an example of a boy's writing in his literacy class.

Pictured top: *These first century probes, needles and sharp hooks are the sort of instruments that Paul's companion, Dr Luke, may have used.*

Pictured above: *Mirrors were made of bronze and were polished until they gave a bright surface to look into.*

FACT BOX:
In the first century, most education was given at home. When a boy went to school he sat on the floor at the feet of his teacher. Girls **never** went to school.

* In *case 3* can you find the 'surgical drill' that would be used to remove arrows? How long do you think it is? ....
* If you went to the doctor and were very poor, how might you pay his fee? The answer is in the picture of the people waiting for treatment.

....

* In *case 7* you can find the piece of pottery on which a child learned to write out his letters. What comes in between each of the consonants? ....
* From this case, name some of the materials they wrote on ....

....

....

Check your answers at the bottom of page 21.

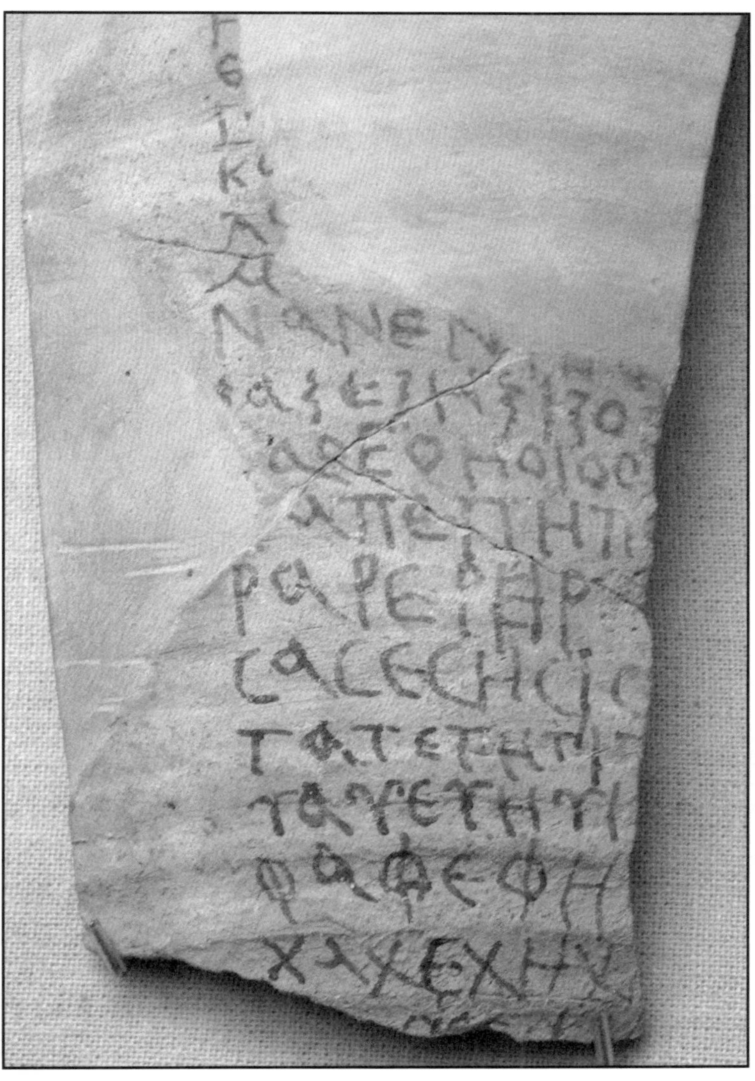

Here is a schoolboy's efforts to write out his Greek alphabet. He used ink, a wooden pen, and a piece of broken pottery. Use a sheet of paper – or even better ask dad or mum for a piece of broken pottery like an old flower pot – and copy some of these letters. You are writing Greek letters, just like this boy did 2,000 years ago.

Do you have anything made of brass in your home? If so, ask mum or dad if you can polish it as clean and as bright as you can — and then look into it. That is all they had for mirrors in the first century. Not as clear as your glass mirrors at home is it?

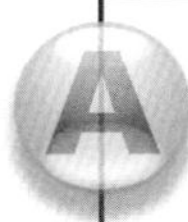

Answers to page 17

- The lamp mould with the Christian symbol on it was made in the fourth or fifth century AD.
- The mask was made between 525 and 500 BC and it was made from terracotta (clay).

SEE THROUGH THE BRITISH MUSEUM WITH THE BIBLE (3RD EDITION) PAGE 106

British Museum Room 69. Cases 4 Greek and Roman dress and 8 Children.

Smelly feet!

The roads were rough and dusty in the first century in the land of Palestine, so what sort of footwear would you expect people to use? Most people either went barefoot or they wore sandals. The Roman soldier had a special kind of sandal that would not wear out quickly. He also had 'hobnailed boots' which were leather boots fitted with nails hammered into the soles to help give him a good grip. Writing to the Christians at Ephesus, the apostle Paul encouraged them to have their feet *'fitted with the readiness'* that comes from what he called *'the gospel of peace'* (Ephesians 6 verse 15). He meant that, like the strong boots of a Roman soldier, they must be ready to take the good news of Jesus wherever God wants them to.

In *case 4* in the Museum there is a small model of the soldier's sandal and a model of his boots with the hobnails in the soles. Guess what these little models were used for? They are scent bottles! If you gave that to a friend as a present, you would be dropping a big hint about smelly feet!

Toys and children

Children played with toys in the first century just as they do today. Girls made their own dolls out of rags or clay, and boys often played with toys to push along. Sometimes when a child died, they would bury toys with it, thinking that the child would be able to play with them in the next world.

Pictured top: *Two small scent bottles in the form of a sandal and a boot of the type worn by Roman soldiers.*

Pictured above: Guess what? *This was made 2,000 years ago. What do you think it is?* (Check your answer on page 23).

FACT BOX:
A Roman soldier was expected to be able to walk 30 kilometres in five hours with his full pack of food, armour and weapons weighing 30 kg.

* In *case 4,* what is the name given to the sandal worn by the Roman soldier?..

* At the end of Room 69 there is something important for you to find in *case 32*. Look for the item with the accession no. GR 1951.6–6.14.

What is it?..

Check your answers at the bottom of page 23.

Who is the toughest soldier?

A Roman soldier had to march 30 kilometres (18½ miles) in 5 hours with a pack weighing 30 kg.

A Royal Marine Commando has to march 55 kilometres (34 miles) in 8 hours with a pack weighing 18 kg.

Who do you think is the toughest soldier?

If you have bathroom scales at home, check out what would make up 30 kg.

It might even be a younger brother or sister! Imagine carrying that weight for 30 kilometres.

Here is a Roman soldier with all his armour and weapons. Colour him in using the picture on the front cover of this book to help you. Then turn to Ephesians 6 verses 13 to 17 and mark on your picture the different parts of the armour that Paul mentions in these verses.

A

Answers to page 19

- The surgical drill is almost 30 cms long. • You might pay your fee with a hare or a rabbit.
- A vowel comes between each consonant.
- Some of the material they wrote on was bone, pottery, wood, papyrus and bronze (brass).

British Museum Room 69. Cases 22 and 23 Music, 9 Games and 24 An Athenian Festival.

Playing games

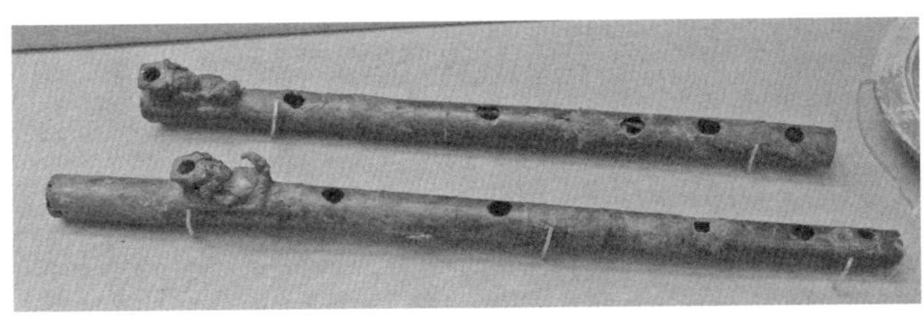

Some of the games we play today are similar to those children were playing two thousand years ago in the time of Jesus. He once spoke about *'children sitting in the market-place and calling out to each other: "We played the flute for you, and you did not dance; we sang a dirge, and you did not cry."'* (Luke 7 verse 32). Those children were obviously playing weddings and funerals! You can find a flute in the Museum.

One game that was very popular was called 'knucklebones'. You may know it as 'five-stones' or some other name. One ancient Greek writer describes the game of knucklebones:

'The knucklebones are thrown up into the air and an attempt is made to catch them on the back of the hand. If you are only partially successful, you have to pick up the knucklebones which have fallen to the ground, without letting fall those already on the hand.'

The writer then adds: 'It is, above all, a game for women'!

If you get your friends to play this game, tell them that kids have been playing 'five-stones' for at least 2,500 years.

Olympics

The people of Athens loved their sports and they held a festival which included athletics, wrestling, boxing, discus and javelin throwing and chariot racing. All of which helped prepare them for battle.

In *case 24* in the Museum there is evidence of some of this. Competitors for the long jump would carry a stone weight in their hand – it weighed 2.23 kg – to give them propulsion when they jumped and a backward thrust just before they landed. Do you think it would help?

FACT BOX:
The Olympic Games were first held at Olympia in Greece in 776 BC. They were held every four years and were intended to entertain the gods and keep them happy. Our modern Olympic Games began in 1894.

Pictured top: *Jesus would have seen flutes like this being played by the children in the streets of Palestine.*

Pictured above: *A pair of jumping weights — one for each hand.*

* In *case 9* there is a picture of two girls playing knucklebones.
  What date is this?..........
* What other games can you find in *case 9*?..........

....

Check your answers at the bottom of page 25.

INVENT A GAME

In the first century the rules for knucklebones could be quite complicated and each stone had its own value. The stones could also be made from wood or bones.

Find five small stones or pieces of wood and play a game with a friend. Often each knucklebone had a different value, so can you improve on the rules given by that ancient Greek writer?

Remember this is a game children have been playing for 2,500 years or more.

Thinking about what you have already learned from this room in the Museum, what sport do you think the boys might be playing whilst their sisters were playing knucklebones?

....

Answers to pages 20 and 21

- The Guess what? object is a baby's bottle feeder. And on the side are the words: 'Drink, don't drop'!
- The sandal worn by a Roman soldier was called a *krepis*
- GR 1951.6–6.14. is a bronze figurine of Artemis (Diana) a goddess worshipped in Ephesus.

British Museum Room 68 HSBC Money Gallery case 3 and 5.

Money with a message

Take a look at a coin in your pocket. It has the Queen's head on one side (this side is called the *obverse* or *head*), and a design on the other side (this side is called the *reverse* or *tail*). People have been using coins as money for nearly three thousand years, but by the time of Jesus, the emperor's head appeared on some of the coins. When Jesus held up a coin and asked, *'Whose portrait is this?'* (Matthew 22 verse 19), the crowd was looking at the portrait of Tiberius. That coin was called a *denarius*.

Silver shekels

A silver *shekel* from Tyre was the main coin used in Judea to pay the tax for the upkeep of the Temple in Jerusalem. One day Jesus sent Peter fishing and when he came back he had found in a fish's mouth a small silver coin called a *stater* and this was worth a whole *shekel* which was enough for both of them (Matthew 17 verse 27).

Pictured above: *Here is a* denarius *just like the one Jesus held up. It has the image of Tiberius and the words 'Divine Augustus' on it. We have given you a big picture, but beside it is its real size. Not very impressive, is it?*

Pictured right: *Here is a* shekel *from Tyre. It was the preferred coin for paying the Temple tax because the silver from Tyre was high quality.*

FACT BOX:
A denarius was the amount a man would earn for one day working on the land. Look up Matthew 20 verse 2 and you will find it there. It was also the daily pay of an ordinary Roman soldier.

* In Room 68 find the *denarius* of Tiberius in *case 3* panel 3.
  What number is it here? ....
* Can you also find two silver *shekels* of Tyre here?
  What numbers do they have? ....
* Can you remember those soldier's boots on page 20 with hobnails in the soles? Now look in *case 5* panel 2. How many hobnails could you buy for two copper coins called an *ass*? To help you, find items numbered 3,4,5.

Check your answers at the bottom of page 27.

HERE IS ANOTHER GAME TO PLAY WITH A FRIEND

You will each need 15 coins; that is, five of each of the coins pictured here. You can photocopy these and cut and paste them on card, or draw them yourself.

The first is the *denarius* coin, the second a *Pilate* coin and the third a *shekel*.

THE RULES OF THE GAME

1. Each player stacks their coins so that their opponent cannot see which one is on top.
2. Taking turns, you have to guess which coin is on top of your opponent's pile. If you guess correctly, your opponent gives you from the top of their pile:
   4 coins for a ***denarius;***
   3 coins for a ***Pilate;***
   2 coins for a ***shekel.***
   The new coins are placed at the bottom of your pile and you have another go.
3. When you guess incorrectly you have to give your top coin to the other player, who places it at the bottom of his pile, and the guessing passes to your opponent who tries to guess your top coin.
4. The first player to gain all the coins is the winner.
5. It could take a long time, so you may want to set a time limit and then see who has the most coins.

Answers to page 23

- The date of the two girls playing knucklebones is 340–330 BC.
- You can also find in case 9: dice, marbles, counters, board games, juggling and hoops.
- The boys would be playing war games.

The British Museum Room 18 The Parthenon Galleries.

How Athens lost its marbles

The Parthenon in Athens was being used as a gunpowder store by the Turkish army and – yes you guessed it – one day the gunpowder blew up and made the ruined Parthenon an even bigger ruin! That was in 1687, but nobody really cared, so in 1801 Lord Elgin took some of the marble sculptures and brought them back to Britain for safe keeping and they are now in the British Museum. That's why they are called 'The Elgin Marbles'.

Around the year AD 50 the Apostle Paul came to Athens (the story is told in Acts 17), and he must have been impressed by the magnificent marble Parthenon towering over the city. Much of it was brilliantly coloured, like the Entrance Hall ceiling in the Museum on page 4. The Parthenon was the temple of Athena, the goddess from whom the city took its name. Every four years her birthday was celebrated by presenting her gold and ivory statue with a fabulous new robe; the ceremony was accompanied by a procession of horsemen with animals being led for sacrifice.

Paul may have seen this procession when he was in the city, but he would certainly have seen the sculptures that are here in the Museum. Paul was amazed at how many gods Athens worshipped and he told them about the true God whom they did not worship (see Acts 17 verses 22 to 23).

Pictured: *The marble sculptures on the frieze in the Parthenon Gallery (the Elgin Marbles) show the procession on the birthday of the goddess Athena.*

FACT BOX:
The Parthenon was right on the top of the Acropolis in Athens. It was built nearly 500 years before Paul arrived in the city, and 500 years after Paul the Parthenon was used as a Christian church before it was finally ruined by an explosion in 1687.

* When was the Parthenon built?..
* Look for the display boards of the Acropolis and Parthenon in the left hand side, Room 18a, before you enter Room 18. What does 'Acropolis' mean? ....

(You can always ask one of the attendants in uniform where it is – they will be glad to help you.)

Check your answers at the bottom of page 29.

Do you want to see what the Parthenon in Athens looks like today? Photocopy this page onto card and then cut out these pieces of a jigsaw and fit them together, then you will see it.

Start arguing!

Do you think Lord Elgin was right to bring these sculptures back to London in 1801? YES/ NO

Can you give two reasons for your answer?

1. ....

2. ....

(If you are in the Museum there is a clue to help you with your answer in the side room on the left, Room 18a. Look for the picture of the 'The Parthenon's later life' on the left hand wall and read what it says. Or you could read the information board on the right and the centre panel called 'controversy'.)

Answers to page 25

- The two *denarius* of Tiberius are numbered 20 and 21.
- The silver *shekels* of Tyre are numbered 22 and 23.
- You could buy 100 hobnails for your boots for two *asses* (that's the name of a coin!)

SEE **THROUGH THE BRITISH MUSEUM WITH THE BIBLE (3RD EDITION)** PAGES 112-113

British Museum Room 22 Greece and Rome.

Four wise men

Athens was proud of its stunning buildings, excellent university and long history of clever men. These men are known as 'philosophers'. When Paul arrived in the city he was soon debating with their followers.

In fact, according to Dr Luke some people seemed to have nothing else to do than discuss philosophy (see Acts 17 verse 21).

In the Museum there is a line-up of four of the great philosophers of ancient Athens.

Epikouros believed that the best way is to enjoy life by freedom from worry and pain. He didn't believe in the supernatural or miracles. He was the founder of the Epicurean philosophy.

Chrysippos believed the opposite of Epikouros and thought that health, happiness and money were irrelevant and even evil. What matters is just to be good and self controlled. He was the founder of the Stoic philosophy.

Antisthenes believed that hard work and honesty were the most important things in life, pleasure was despised. He was the founder of the Cynic philosophy.

Socrates had the most brilliant mind Athens ever produced and was eventually forced to commit suicide because his clever brain made others look silly. Socrates believed the best way of life was to trust in yourself and try to find what is good.

Paul got talking about Jesus Christ with the followers of these wise men, but soon *'Some of them asked, "What is this babbler trying to say?" Others remarked, "He seems to be advocating foreign gods." They said this because Paul was preaching the good news about Jesus and the resurrection.'* (Acts 17 verse 18). Some of them 'sneered' at him (verse 32) and these were probably the Cynics.

Pictured: *The four philosophers of Athens. From right to left: Epikouros, Chrysippos, Antisthenes and Socrates. They had all died long before Paul arrived, but their followers were still in the city.*

FACT BOX:
The word 'philosophy' comes from two Greek words that mean 'a love of wisdom'.

* In Room 22, look for the plaque called 'Portraits of Greek philosophers' beside the four wise men. The busts of Antisthenes and Epikouros were found on the main road leading to Rome. What was it called?

....

* Look up Acts 17 verse 18 in the New Testament. Two of these philosophies are mentioned there, which two are **NOT**?

....

Check your answer at the bottom of page 31.

Here are three new words to learn from three of those philosophers — the Epicureans, the Stoics and the Cynics:

An 'epicure' is a person with very good taste, especially in food and drink.
A 'stoic' is a person with complete self control in pain and suffering.
A 'cynic' is a person who has very little trust in other human beings.

Write out a sentence below the bust of each wise man that contains his word and will show its meaning. Be careful, the philosophers here are not in the same order as on the previous page!

What was the message of Paul that so upset some of the followers of these wise men?
(Acts 17 verse 18).

'_ _'

Answers to page 27

- The Parthenon was built between 447 and 432 BC. Interestingly, this was just after the Jews finished rebuilding the Temple in Jerusalem in the time of Ezra and Nehemiah whose stories are in the Bible.
- Acropolis means 'High City'.

British Museum Room 22 Greece and Rome.

Diana of the Ephesians!

One day long, long ago, an image of the Greek goddess Diana fell from the sky and landed in the city of Ephesus, so the inhabitants built a small shrine to protect her image — well, that's what the Ephesians believed. Soon a temple was built, and when that burnt down, an even more magnificent one was built. It was all of marble and had 100 huge columns to hold up the roof; 36 were carved with figures of other gods.

Reach out both your arms sideways as far as you can — the diameter of each column was three times more than that!

Diana is the Latin name for the goddess known in Greek as Artemis. The Ephesians were very proud of Diana, and people came from all over the Roman empire to worship at her magnificent temple. It was a thriving tourist industry and the silversmiths made lots of money selling little statuettes of Diana to the visitors.

When Paul arrived in Ephesus (the story is in Acts 19), he began telling people about Jesus Christ; so many people believed, that the silversmiths saw their trade threatened, and as a result they started a riot. The crowds shouted 'Great is Artemis of the Ephesians!' Fortunately the chief man of the city was able to stop the riot and the next day Paul and Silas left to travel to Macedonia. But Christians began worshipping the true God in Ephesus.

The worship of Diana has long since disappeared, but the good news that Paul preached is now all over the world.

Pictured: *This little statuette of the goddess Diana is similar to those made by the silversmiths in the time of Paul. This one is in case 32 in room 69 and is only a few centimetres high.*

FACT BOX:
Today, there is almost nothing left of the temple of Diana apart from a single column in a muddy pool in Ephesus and the base of the column that you can see in the British Museum.

SEARCH BOX

* Room 22 contains the only known sculptured column anywhere from the Temple of Diana. Tick here when you have seen it ☐.
* Close by is the bust of Alexander the Great who lived 300 years before Jesus Christ was born. Can you find him? Alexander ruled over three million square miles of the earth and this is why much of the world spoke Greek by the time Jesus of Nazareth was born; this made the spread of the Christian message much easier.
* In *case 2* look for coin no 14. It has on it an image of Alexander's famous white horse. What was its name? ....

Check your answer at the bottom of this page.

If you were a silversmith in Ephesus, write in one sentence what would you accuse Paul of?

____

____

What do you think Paul would say in his defence?

____

____

THIS IS A TOUGH ONE!

In a letter to the Christians at Corinth, Paul told them about some of his suffering for preaching about Jesus. Find out what happened to him by rearranging the letters. You can look up **2 Corinthians 11verses 23 and 25** to check your answers.

N E D O S T   T E A N E B   D E G G F L O   C H E D E K W I S P R

_ _ _ _ _ _   _ _ _ _ _ _   _ _ _ _ _ _ _   _ _ _ _ _ _ _ _ _ _ _

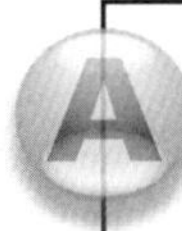

Answers to page 29

- They were found near the Via Appia, south of Rome. Paul would have travelled this road on his journey to Rome recorded in Acts 28.
- The Cynics and Socrates are not mentioned by name.
- 'Jesus and the resurrection' (Acts 17 verse 18).

Answer to SEARCH BOX on this page

The name of Alexander's horse was Boukephalos.

Timeline from Jesus to the emperor Titus

This timeline includes only those names mentioned in this activity book. The dates for the birth and death of Jesus Christ are approximate.

DATE	WHAT HAPPENED?
BC	
54	Julius Caesar first landed in Britain.
27	Caesar Augustus became the first Roman emperor.
5	Jesus Christ was born.
AD	
14	Tiberius became emperor.
30	The death and resurrection of Jesus Christ.
41	Claudius became emperor.
43	Roman armies landed in Britain and won all the land up to the River Thames.
44	The apostle Paul began his missionary journeys.
54	Nero became emperor.
61	The revolt and defeat of Queen Boudica in Britain.
64	The Great Fire of Rome and the execution of the apostle Paul in Rome.
69	Vespasian became emperor.
70	The siege and destruction of Jerusalem by Titus the Roman general.
79	Titus became emperor.

Day One Publications 2008 Second Edition 2013

A Catalogue record is held at The British Library ISBN 978-1-84625-036-1

Published by Day One Publications, Ryelands Road, Leominster HR6 8NZ

☎ 01568 613 740 FAX 01568 611 472 email—sales@dayone.co.uk www.dayone.co.uk

Series Editor: Brian Edwards

Design and Art Direction: Wild Associates Ltd

Printed by Orchard Press Cheltenham Ltd